BRINGING BACK THE
Island Fox

Rachel Stuckey

Crabtree Publishing Company
www.crabtreebooks.com

CRABTREE
PUBLISHING COMPANY
WWW.CRABTREEBOOKS.COM

Author: Rachel Stuckey

Series Research and Development: Reagan Miller

Picture Manager: Sophie Mortimer

Design Manager: Keith Davis

Editorial Director: Lindsey Lowe

Children's Publisher: Anne O'Daly

Editor: Ellen Rodger

Proofreader: Crystal Sikkens

Cover design: Margaret Amy Salter

**Production coordinator and
  Prepress technician:** Margaret Amy Salter

Print coordinator: Katherine Berti

Produced for Crabtree Publishing Company
by Brown Bear Books

Photographs
(t=top, b= bottom, l=left, r=right, c=center)

Front Cover: All images from Shutterstock

Interior: Alamy: Gary Crabbe 16, Kip Evans 29, Nik Wheeler
10; Catalina Island Conservancy: 21b; Friends of the Channel
Island Fox: 28; Getty Images: Los Angeles Times/Stephen
Osman 23; iStock: Ayimages 27b, benedek 15, Jeff Goulden
27t, Igorkov 9b, JStewartphoto 4, 7, Gary Kavanagh 5b, Nick
Lust Photography 20, Kyle T Perry 1, wrangel 6; National
Park Service: 14b, 18, 19, 21t, 22, David Garcelon 14cr: Nature
Picture Library: Ch'ien C. Lee 8, Minden Pictures/Jaymi
Heimbuch 24, Kevin Schafer 26; Public Domain: unknown 9t,
Shutterstock: 13, Ian Duffield 17; Stock Adobe: Chuck/Sonya
Van Dam 5t; U.S. Fish and Wildlife Service: 12.

Brown Bear Books has made every attempt to contact the
copyright holder. If you have any information please contact
licensing@brownbearbooks.co.uk

Library and Archives Canada Cataloguing in Publication

Title: Bringing back the island fox / Rachel Stucky.
Names: Stuckey, Rachel, author.
Series: Animals back from the brink.
Description: Series statement: Animals back from the brink |
  Includes index.
Identifiers: Canadiana (print) 20190233397 |
  Canadiana (ebook) 20190233400 |
  ISBN 9780778768197 (hardcover) |
  ISBN 9780778768418 (softcover) |
  ISBN 9781427124272 (HTML)
Subjects: LCSH: Urocyon—Channel Islands—Juvenile literature. |
  LCSH: Urocyon—Conservation—Channel Islands—Juvenile literature.
  | LCSH: Foxes—Channel Islands—Juvenile literature. | LCSH:
  Foxes—Conservation—Channel Islands—Juvenile literature. |
  LCSH: Endangered species—Channel Islands—Juvenile literature. |
  LCSH: Wildlife recovery—Channel Islands—Juvenile literature.
Classification: LCC QL737.C22 S78 2020 | DDC j599.77609423/4—dc23

Library of Congress Cataloging-in-Publication Data

Names: Stuckey, Rachel, author.
Title: Bringing back the island fox / Rachel Stuckey.
Other titles: Animals back from the brink.
Description: New York, New York : Crabtree Publishing Company,
  [2020] | Series: Animals back from the brink |
  Includes bibliographical references and index.
Identifiers: LCCN 2019053199 (print) | LCCN 2019053200 (ebook) |
  ISBN 9780778768197 (hardcover) | ISBN 9780778768418 (paperback) |
  ISBN 9781427124272 (ebook)
Subjects: LCSH: Urocyon--Conservation--Juvenile literature. | Foxes--
  Conservation--Juvenile literature. | Wildlife conservation--California--
  Channel Islands--Juvenile literature.
Classification: LCC QL737.C22 S789 2020 (print) |
  LCC QL737.C22 (ebook) | DDC 599.776--dc23
LC record available at https://lccn.loc.gov/2019053199
LC ebook record available at https://lccn.loc.gov/2019053200

Crabtree Publishing Company

www.crabtreebooks.com   1-800-387-7650

Printed in the U.S.A./022020/CG20200102

Published in Canada
Crabtree Publishing
616 Welland Ave.
St. Catharines, Ontario
L2M 5V6

Published in the United States
Crabtree Publishing
PMB 59051
350 Fifth Avenue, 59th Floor
New York, New York 10118

Published in the United Kingdom
Crabtree Publishing
Maritime House
Basin Road North, Hove
BN41 1WR

Published in Australia
Crabtree Publishing
Unit 3–5 Currumbin Court
Capalaba
QLD 4157

Contents

Saving the Island Foxes

The Channel Islands off California are home to the second smallest foxes in the world. They are about 20 inches (50 cm) long, and 12 inches (30 cm) tall, and have a tail that is 4 to 11 inches (10 to 28 cm) long. There are six **subspecies** of island fox, each unique to a particular island in the **archipelago**. The first foxes were descended from the mainland gray fox. Scientists think these foxes traveled to the northern islands from the mainland on floating logs over 10,000 years ago. Until the mid-1990s, the fox populations were stable. However, a rapid increase in the golden eagle population had a disastrous effect on the island foxes.

The largest of the island foxes live on Santa Catalina Island. The smallest live on Santa Cruz Island. All the island foxes have gray fur on their heads and their backs, red fur on the sides of their necks and down their legs, and white fur on their throats, chests, and bellies.

ISLAND FOX FACTS

Island foxes are at their most active during dawn and dusk. They eat fruit, insects, birds, eggs, crabs, lizards, and small mammals such as deer mice. They have a short lifespan, living for only four to six years in the wild and up to eight years in captivity, although some individuals have lived for up to 15 years. **Breeding pairs** mate between January and March and produce two or three pups in the spring. By the summer, young foxes are ready to leave the den. At 10 months of age, young foxes are ready to have their own pups.

Annual rainfall on the California Channel Islands is low. As a result, the native island vegetation is mostly scrubland, with grasses and short, woody plants that do not use much water.

Species at Risk

Created in 1984, the International Union for the **Conservation** of Nature (IUCN) protects wildlife, plants, and natural resources around the world. Its members include about 1,400 governments and nongovernmental organizations. The IUCN publishes the Red List of Threatened **Species** each year, which tells people how likely a plant or animal species is to become **extinct**. It began publishing the list in 1964.

The scimitar-horned oryx has not been seen in the wild in Africa since the 1990s. In 2016, the IUCN officially listed it as Extinct in the Wild (EX).

SCIENTIFIC CRITERIA

The Red List, created by scientists, divides nearly 80,000 species of plants and animals into nine categories. Criteria for each category include the growth and decline of the population size of a species. They also include how many individuals within a species can breed, or have babies. In addition, scientists include information about the **habitat** of the species, such as its size and quality. These criteria allow scientists to figure out the probability of extinction facing the species.

IUCN LEVELS OF THREAT

The Red List uses nine categories to define the threat to a species.

Extinct (EX)	No living individuals survive.
Extinct in the Wild (EW)	Species cannot be found in its natural habitat. Exists only in **captivity**, in **cultivation**, or in an area that is not its natural habitat.
Critically Endangered (CR)	At extremely high risk of becoming extinct in the wild.
Endangered (EN)	At very high risk of extinction in the wild.
Vulnerable (VU)	At high risk of extinction in the wild.
Near Threatened (NT)	Likely to become threatened in the near future.
Least Concern (LC)	Widespread, abundant, or at low risk.
Data Deficient (DD)	Not enough data to make a judgment about the species.
Not Evaluated (NE)	Not yet evaluated against the criteria.

he United States,
Endangered Species
of 1973 was passed
protect species from
ssible extinction.
as its own criteria for
ssifying species, but
y are similar to those
he IUCN. Canada
oduced the Species
Risk Act in 2002.
re than 530 species
protected under the
. The list of species
ompiled by the
mmittee on the Status
ndangered Wildlife
Canada (COSEWIC).

ISLAND FOXES AT RISK

In the 1990s, island fox populations fell dramatically. The island foxes were classed as endangered under the U.S. Endangered Species Act. On San Miguel Island, population numbers fell from 450 in 1994 to just 15 in 1999. In 1994, there were 2,000 Santa Cruz Island foxes, but by the year 2000, numbers had fallen to 135. The population on Santa Rosa Island also fell, from 1,500 to 14. Following Conservation efforts, the IUCN Red List classified all island foxes as Near Threatened (NT) in 2013.

Threats to Survival

Island foxes had been the main **predators** on their remote islands for thousands of years. Few humans lived on the islands, and the fox populations had remained undisturbed and healthy. However, in the 1990s, populations began a steep decline. The foxes were facing major threats to their survival.

Invasive species were the biggest threat. In the 1850s, farmers had introduced pigs to the islands. Within 100 years, **feral** pigs had overtaken the habitat, competing for space with the smaller population of foxes. The pigs provided a food source for the newly arrived golden eagles, which also threatened the small island foxes.

In 1998, the fox population on Santa Catalina was almost wiped out by canine distemper, a virus carried by pet dogs that affects related animals such as prairie dogs, ferrets, and foxes. Ninety percent of the foxes on the island died.

HUMAN THREAT

In the 1930s, scientists discovered that a chemical known as DDT was useful for killing insects. This poison was used during World War II to control the spread of diseases such as malaria and typhoid, which are carried by mosquitoes. DDT saved many lives, but it was also used on the land by farmers. The poisons built up in the environment and had a negative effect on humans and animals. DDT is a **toxin** that interferes with reproduction and may also cause cancer. In 1972, the United States banned DDT. However, by that time it had affected the balance of the **ecosystem** on the Channel Islands.

CROSS COUNTRY

insect spray

CONTAINING 50% DDT
RE. PATENT NO. 22,922

destroys many common insects

USE ON POTATOES, PEAS, CORN, FRUITS and ORNAMENTALS

No. 1365

NET CONTENTS 1 LB.

POISONING THE FOOD CHAIN

DDT was made at a factory near Los Angeles, California. Between 1947 and 1961, sludge containing hundreds of metric tons of DDT poisoned the fish that the bald eagles on the Channel Islands ate. The DDT made it difficult for the eagles to have chicks. By the 1960s, there were no bald eagles left nesting on the Channel Islands. They had previously frightened off the invasive golden eagles. Once the bald eagles had gone, the golden eagles moved into the islands. They preyed on small land mammals such as foxes.

Balancing the Ecosystem

Invasive species are a major threat to island life. They upset the delicate balance of island ecosystems. Land animals cannot leave an island to look for a better habitat or new food sources. When something happens to alter the environment on an island, all living things are affected. Invasive species not only change the food chain, they also bring disease. Island foxes had not been exposed to diseases and so did not have the same **immunity** as animals on the mainland. Contact with other animals exposed them to disease.

Santa Cruz Island is within the Channel Islands National Park. It is California's largest island and has the greatest variety of plant and animal species of all the islands.

PORTRAIT OF THE CHANNEL ISLANDS

The Channel Islands are in the Pacific Ocean, off the coast of Santa Barbara, a city just north of Los Angeles. Six of the islands have their own native fox populations. Before the Spanish explorers arrived in California in the 1540s, Native Americans had lived on the islands, but the European settlers forced them to leave. The islands were taken over by farmers, ranchers, and whalers, but few people lived there permanently. Today, the United States military uses some of the islands as training grounds and for testing weapons. Santa Catalina is now the only island to have a permanent human population. The other islands are military bases, research facilities, conservation land, national parks, and camping grounds.

THE CALIFORNIA CHANNEL ISLANDS

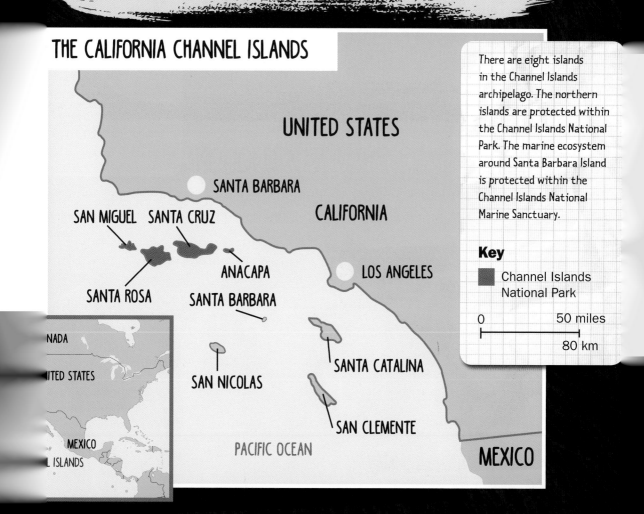

There are eight islands in the Channel Islands archipelago. The northern islands are protected within the Channel Islands National Park. The marine ecosystem around Santa Barbara Island is protected within the Channel Islands National Marine Sanctuary.

Key

■ Channel Islands National Park

0   50 miles

80 km

UNITED STATES

SANTA BARBARA

CALIFORNIA

SAN MIGUEL   SANTA CRUZ

ANACAPA

LOS ANGELES

SANTA ROSA

SANTA BARBARA

SANTA CATALINA

SAN NICOLAS

SAN CLEMENTE

PACIFIC OCEAN

MEXICO

NADA

ITED STATES

MEXICO

L ISLANDS

Who Got Involved?

In the late 1990s, many different conservation groups began to work together to save the island foxes. The Nature Conservancy, the Catalina Island Conservancy, the Institute for Wildlife Studies, and the National Park Service came together to work with the California Department of Fish & Wildlife and the U.S. Fish & Wildlife Service. The Nature Conservancy is the largest environmental nonprofit organization in the Americas. It has successfully protected over 100 million acres (40 million ha) of land and thousands of miles of rivers. The conservancy also works with governments to educate young people and support scientific research in conservation and **biodiversity**.

The Island Fox recovery team included biologists, ecologists, and officials from all the major U.S. wildlife conservation groups. Tim Coonan (second from left) had been one of the first people to notice the decline of the species before they were even listed as endangered. He played a key role in the recovery program.

ISLAND FOX WORKING GROUP

A working group is a group of people who get together to study a particular problem and then make recommendations about what can be done to solve it. Working groups allow different organizations and teams with different areas of expertise to coordinate their actions. The working group holds regular meetings with the organizations to monitor their results. The Island Fox Working Group included landowners, academics, and nonprofit organizations dedicated to saving the island fox. Together, they helped to develop the U.S. Fish & Wildlife Service's official recovery plan for the island foxes.

WHO OWNS THE ISLANDS?

The Channel Island fox recovery plan was able to go into action quickly because the members of the working group had almost total control of the environment. Most of the Channel Islands are owned by four major landowners: the National Park Service (NPS), the U.S. Navy (Navy), The Nature Conservancy (TNC), and the Santa Catalina Island Conservancy (CIC). The National Park Service, The Nature Conservancy, and the Catalina Island Conservancy manage islands where the endangered subspecies live. San Miguel Island is owned by the Navy, but because it is part of the Channel Islands National Park, the land is managed by the park service.

What Was the Plan?

The Channel Island fox recovery plan had two main goals. One was to remove the invasive species to rebalance the ecosystem. The other was to increase the remaining fox population. First, the feral pigs were removed to increase the habitat available for the foxes and to reduce the food supply for the golden eagles. The golden eagles were captured and released away from the islands to remove the foxes' predator. The native American bald eagle was brought back to help keep the golden eagles away. Bald eagles feed on fish, so are no threat to island foxes. Captive breeding was introduced to increase fox numbers. Finally, conservationists watched the population closely to avoid another crisis.

Nesting pairs of American bald eagles had abandoned the Channel Islands in the 1960s. Returning bald eagles to the islands was part of the fox recovery plan. This eagle was released on the islands in 2004.

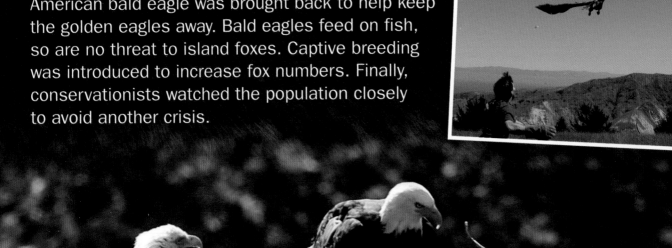

Yellow coreopsis plants flower on Anacapa Island in the spring. The plants provide shelter for nesting birds. The island foxes help to maintain plants that keep the ecosystem in balance. Foxes eat plant seeds and spread them across the island in their waste. New plants grow where the seeds take root.

KEYSTONE FOXES

When other plants and animals in an ecosystem depend on a single species, that species is known as a keystone species. The term "keystone" comes from its use in architecture. The stone at the top of an arch is called a "key stone." If it is removed, the arch will collapse. In nature, if a keystone species is removed from an ecosystem, the ecosystem will change completely. Channel Island foxes are predators at the top of the island food chain. They are the only **carnivores** unique to California. On the islands, foxes help to keep the mouse and skunk population under control. Without the foxes, other animal populations would become large and eat too many plants and birds' eggs.

Removing the Invaders

The first steps in the Channel Island fox recovery plan were to remove the invading species. The Nature Conservancy had observed that feral pigs were a particular problem on Santa Cruz Island. Unlike foxes, pigs are not predators. They did not help to keep the ecosystem in balance. The fox recovery working group considered many solutions to the pig problem. In the end, they decided the best answer was to hunt them. In 2005, the Nature Conservancy hired a team of professional hunters from New Zealand. Santa Cruz was fenced off into sections. The hunters shot from a long distance, often from helicopters, using non-lead bullets to avoid contaminating the environment. Experts made sure the animals suffered no pain.

Some people objected to hunting feral pigs on the islands. Other people thought using skilled hunters would mean the animals would not suffer. They believed that hunting the large population of around 5,000 pigs was the best way to protect the ecosystem and save the island foxes from extinction.

DEALING WITH GOLDEN EAGLES

The feral pigs were an invasive species and their population grew quickly. They attracted a new predator to the islands. Golden eagles had started to arrive in the 1990s. They preyed on small mammals such as pigs and foxes. The island foxes had never had a predator before and didn't fear them. They made an easy target for the predatory eagles. Researchers discovered the remains of foxes near golden eagle nests. The fox population began to fall quickly. However, under the United States Bald and Golden Eagle Protection Act of 1962, golden eagles were protected and could not be hunted. Instead, conservationists had to capture the golden eagles. It took seven years to capture and relocate every golden eagle that had nested on the islands.

Captive Breeding

After they had begun to solve the problem of feral pigs and golden eagles, the working group launched captive breeding programs to increase the fox populations. Each fox subspecies on each island had its own breeding program. It was safer to keep the foxes on their own islands, rather than moving them to breed on the mainland. Moving them might have exposed them to new diseases. Breeding began on San Miguel and Santa Rosa in 2000, and Santa Catalina in 2001. In 2002, a breeding program was started on Santa Cruz to prevent the island's fox population of around 135 individuals from falling as low as populations on San Miguel and Santa Rosa.

Captive breeding pens protected the foxes from golden eagles. The first male and female foxes were taken into captivity just before the mating season and put together in pairs. As pups were born and reached breeding age, computer data helped ensure paired up foxes were not related.

COLLABORATING FOR A CAUSE

Tim Coonan worked for the Channel Islands National Park. He was one of the first researchers to notice that island foxes were in trouble. He started to plan for their recovery before the subspecies was even listed as endangered. Coonan is the biologist responsible for the captive breeding program on the islands. He also represented the Park Service in the working group for island fox recovery. After retiring from the National Park Service, Coonan continued to work on Channel Island fox conservation.

BRINGING BACK THE BALD EAGLES

An important step for balancing the Channel Island ecosystem was the effort to save the American bald eagle. Bald eagles do not eat the same food as golden eagles, but they are competitors for habitat. Bald eagles are very territorial, which means they will not allow other eagle species to nest nearby. However, by the 1950s, bald eagles had stopped breeding on the Channel Islands. Researchers later discovered this was because of DDT pollution. Since the 1960s, conservationists all over the United States have been working to save the bald eagle. Captive breeding programs were set up, and bald eagles were first reintroduced to the islands in the 1980s. However, these birds struggled to survive because of the DDT that had built up in the environment. More birds needed to be raised in captivity.

Success Stories

By 2006, hunters had removed more than 5,000 pigs from the islands. The main food source of the golden eagles had gone. By 2000, 13 golden eagles had been captured and relocated to the mainland. Another 18 were removed by 2004. However, the birds quickly learned to keep away from humans. The conservancy team had to find new ways of capturing the remaining eagles. They used a helicopter to get close to a bird, then used a net gun, which launched a large net over the bird in mid-flight. The last breeding pair of golden eagles was caught this way in June 2004.

The golden eagles that were captured were released in the Sierra Mountains. Their chicks, or eaglets, were sent to the San Diego Zoo where they were raised to adulthood before being released into the wild.

COLLABORATING FOR A CAUSE

Channel Island foxes had never been bred in captivity before. The National Park Service worked closely with California zoos, the Association of Zoos and Aquariums, and other national experts to design the breeding program. They built special centers and made a plan for protecting **genetic diversity**.

In 2004, there were 38 foxes in captivity on San Miguel Island and 46 on Santa Rosa Island, with only seven in the wild. Santa Cruz had a stable wild population of around 100 foxes, with another 25 in the breeding center. Populations began to increase. In 2016, the U.S. Fish & Wildlife Service removed the foxes on these three islands from the endangered species list. The IUCN lists them as Near Threatened (NT).

There are now arou
adult foxes living ir
across the Channel
island's population
survival rate. Howe
foxes will always be
any changes in thei

Return of the Bald Eagle

Scientists and conservationists in the United States started working to save the American bald eagle in the 1960s. On the Channel Islands, the Institute for Wildlife Studies began a program to release bald eagles back on to Santa Catalina Island in the 1980s. But the levels of DDT poisoning were still too high, and these eagles struggled to nest and breed. From 1997, scientists began a creative program to breed bald eagles in captivity so that healthy eagles could be released back into the island population. The program was a success. Since 2006, 129 chicks have hatched on the islands and there are over 20 healthy breeding pairs.

Research ecologist Peter Sharpe helped with island fox research on several of the California Channel Islands. In 1997, he began collecting bald eagle eggs from the islands. These were transported to the San Francisco Zoo to be hatched.

HATCHING BALD EAGLES IN CAPTIVITY

The DDT that remained in the environment had made the eagle egg shells weak. For this reason, bald eagles on the Channel Islands needed help to breed. Biologists removed eggs from wild nests and replaced them with artificial eggs so that the eagles continued to prepare for their chick to hatch. The team **incubated** the eggs in a laboratory. When the chicks hatched, they were put back into the nests and the artificial eggs were removed. Since 1989, 38 chicks have been returned to nests on Catalina Island. As DDT levels have fallen, the population is now breeding in the wild.

"HACKING" EAGLES

As part of the bald eagle recovery program, eaglets were hatched and reared at the Avian Conservation Center at the San Francisco Zoo. Wild-born eaglets were also collected from wild nests in Juneau, Alaska, where the eagle population was stable. Releasing eagles into the wild is called "hacking." The birds are released from tall hacking towers on the islands. Each tower has a number of cages where young bald eagles are kept for a few weeks until they are ready to fly. The young eagles are also fed the type of foods they will be eating in the wild. The eagles are watched on closed circuit TV (CCTV) to make sure they are eating and behaving normally. Since 2002, the Institute for Wildlife Studies has released over 60 American bald eagles on Santa Cruz Island.

What Does the Future Hold?

Thanks to a dedicated team, the Channel Island foxes have had the fastest population recovery in wildlife history. This was only possible because the Channel Islands are a controlled ecosystem, with limited human development. But the foxes still face threats. Their small populations make them very vulnerable. Some experts have suggested that the different subspecies should be moved between islands. Allowing these closely related subspecies to interbreed will improve their genetic diversity. If one island's population shrinks, foxes could be reintroduced from other islands to balance the population. However, there are no current plans to interbreed the island foxes.

The different organizations managing the Channel Islands keep close watch on the foxes. They use radio collars to track and locate young foxes. Foxes are also captured for medical examinations. Each fox is vaccinated against rabies and canine distemper.

FRIENDS OF THE ISLAND FOX

Now that the Channel Island fox populations have recovered and are becoming stable, the focus is on protection and conservation. Friends of the Island Fox is a group of conservation professionals and private citizens. This group helps to raise public awareness about the foxes. They also raise funds to support education, research, and conservation programs. The group provides education programs to community groups and schools, from kindergarten through college.

CHANNEL ISLAND FOX POPULATIONS 1994-2018

In 2018, there were unseasonably high temperatures on the Channel Islands. There was also very little rainfall. The hot, dry weather reduced the survival rate of both adult foxes and their new pups. However, in spring 2019, California had heavier than normal rainfall, ending the state's seven-year drought. Experts hope this will improve the survival rate in the coming years, although wildfires and threats to food supplies remain a problem.

Legend:
- Santa Cruz
- Santa Rosa
- Santa Catalina
- San Clemente
- San Nicolas
- San Miguel

Line graph: NUMBER OF FOXES (y-axis, 0 to 3,000) vs. DATE (x-axis, 1994 to 2018)

Saving Other Species

Lessons learned in the fight to save the Channel Island foxes could be used to protect or save other endangered canine species.

Darwin's Fox lives on mainland Chile in the Nahuelbuta National Park and the Valdivian Coastal Range. It also lives on Chiloé Island and suffers from threats that are similar to those suffered by the Channel Island foxes. The biggest of these is canine distemper, which Darwin's Foxes catch from feral dogs. The dogs also attack them. The destruction of their forest habitat is another threat to their survival. If numbers continue to fall, captive breeding programs may be used to protect against extinction of the species.

In 2016, Darwin's Fox was classified as Endangered (EN) on the IUCN Red List. The IUCN estimates the number of adult foxes of breeding age is between 659 and 2,400, with the population currently falling.

RED WOLF

The red wolf once ranged from the southeastern United States northward into Canada. Numbers fell drastically due to habitat loss for human development, the effects of **climate change**, and illegal killings. By 1980, the red wolf was classified as Extinct in the Wild (EX). Although the U.S. Fish & Wildlife Service began a reintroduction program, numbers have fallen to between 20 and 30 breeding age individuals in a small area of North Carolina. In 2018, the IUCN Red List classified the red wolf as Critically Endangered (CR).

DHOLE

The dhole, also called the Asian dog, is a native species of Southeast Asia. Their numbers have fallen due to hunting by farmers and loss of their natural habitat. Dholes live in the rainforests, but much of this habitat has been destroyed over the last 50 years in favor of land clearance for palm oil, paper, and rubber, or for mining and farming. This has also resulted in a lack of food sources for the dhole. There are currently no conservation programs. In 2015, with the number of mature individuals estimated at between 950 and 2,200, the IUCN Red List classified the dhole as Endangered (EN).

What Can You Do to Help?

The Channel Island foxes are back from the brink of extinction, but they are still at risk. Why not become an Island Fox Ambassador? This program is run by the Friends of the Island Fox, and shows young people how to play an active part by raising money to save the island foxes. You, your class, grade, or school could raise money by holding bake sales or quizzes. The money helps volunteers to carry on their work.

Raising money is a great way to help the Channel Island foxes. The money helps to pay for medicines, radio collars, and microchips. These are all things needed to make sure the island fox populations stay healthy and protected.

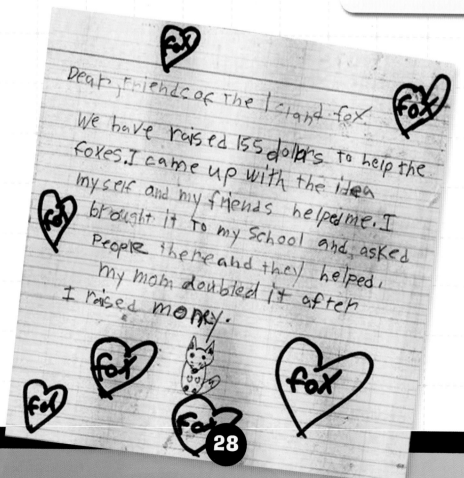

Dear, Friends of the Island fox. We have raised 155 dollars to help the foxes. I came up with the idea myself and my friends helped me. I brought it to my School and, asked People there and they helped, my mom doubled it after I raised money.

Keeping all beaches clean and clear of plastic and other harmful objects that pollute the oceans helps to protect island wildlife.

SPREAD THE WORD

As well as spreading information and educating people, here are some other great ideas for things you could do to help the island foxes:

- Make sure your pet dogs are vaccinated against rabies and canine distemper, particularly if you live near wild places where foxes live.

- Write your elected representative or local newspaper and ask them to support the organizations working to stop **global warming**. Drought caused by global warming makes it difficult for island foxes to find enough food.

- Do what you can to help keep waterways clean. Storm drains, streams, and rivers drain into the oceans, and any polluted water damages ecosystems and the animals that depend on them.

- Prepare and show a PowerPoint presentation to your class explaining how the Channel Island foxes were saved from the brink of extinction.

Learning More

Books

Heyning Laverty, Corinne. *North America's Galapagos: The Historic Channel Islands Biological Survey.* University of Utah Press, 2020.

King, Julie, and Dawn Navarro Ericson, et al. *Island Fox: California's Archipelago.* Manta Publications, 2013.

Siber, Kate, and Chris Turnham. *National Parks of the U.S.A.* Wide Eyed Editions, 2018.

Steiner, Christina. *Shimji, The Channel Island Vixen.* Outskirts Press, 2017.

On the Web

www1.islandfox.org/

This is the Friends of the Island Fox website. It features news pages, current population statistics, features, and information on individual foxes. Also includes several videos.

www.nps.gov/chis/learn/nature/island-fox.htm

Pages on the island foxes from the National Parks Service website. Includes a video on restoring the balance of plants and wildlife on Santa Cruz Island.

www.sbzoo.org/animal/island-fox/

Great website from the Santa Barbara Zoo with pages on the story of the Channel Island foxes. Wonderful map and photographs, plus a video showing two orphaned pups (Lewis and Clark) that were rescued from San Clemente Island.

www.nps.gov/chis/learn/nature/bald-eagles.htm

Pages on the bald eagle and its importance to the island foxes. Includes a video on the story of restoring the bald eagle to the Channel Islands.

https://www.islandconservation.org/npr-skunk-bear-recovery-channel-island-fox/

Watch a video to learn more about the recovery of the Channel Island fox on Santa Cruz Island.

Glossary

archipelago A group of islands close to each other

biodiversity The variety of living things in an ecosystem or the world

breeding pairs A female and male of an animal that mate and have offspring

captivity Being confined for various reasons

carnivores Animals that eat other animals

climate change A change in normal global weather patterns

conservation The preserving and protecting of plants, animals, and natural resources

cultivation Animals or plants that are raised or grown with human help

ecosystem All living things in an area and how they interact

extinct Describes a situation in which all members of a species have died, so the species no longer exists

feral Animals that were once pets but now live in the wild

genetic diversity When a species has a variety of genes in its population

global warming The gradual increase of the average temperature on Earth

habitat The natural surroundings in which an animal lives

immunity The ability of a living thing to resist a virus or infection

incubated Kept eggs warm to create the best conditions for hatching

invasive species A species that is not native to an ecosystem, and which causes damage to the natural plants and animals in the area

predators Animals that naturally prey on or hunt other animals for food

species A group of similar animals or plants that can breed with one another

subspecies A species within a group, but which has different or unique features

toxin A poisonous substance usually produced within living cells or organisms

Index and About the Author

ABOUT THE AUTHOR

Rachel Stuckey is a writer and editor with over 15 years of experience in educational publishing. She has written 30 books for young readers on topics ranging from science to sports, and works with subject matter experts to develop educational resources in both the sciences and humanities. Rachel travels for half the year, working on projects while exploring the world and learning about our global community.